The Greatest Gift OF All

Written by Charleen M. Huyler
Illustrated by Ammar Arshad

The Bible verse, Luke 2:11, mentioned in this book is from the New International Version.

It was a month before Christmas, and all was quite busy as Victoria scurried around the house and garden with eagle eyes. The much-anticipated scavenger hunt leading up to Christmas Day had begun! Victoria was good at locating hidden gifts based on clues, and this year was no different.

As the weeks passed, Victoria amassed an amazing twenty gifts for cracking twenty clues! This was very exciting to Victoria because the gifts would allow her to make more Christmas donations to the local charity for children.

Mom had prepared a special area in the house to showcase all the wonderful items Victoria collected from the hunt. The hunt was created around the events leading up to and around the Christmas story and the very special baby boy that was born in a manger many, many years ago.

It was December twenty-fourth, and the Christmas scavenger hunt was nearing its much-anticipated finale.

Victoria was given the final clue to lead her to the final gift. She carefully opened the clue sheet and gasped! The page was empty!

Victoria's godmother, Bernice, who was the mastermind behind the monthlong event, had extended the suspense! Victoria looked at Mom with wide eyes and an unspoken question—*How do I find my last Christmas scavenger hunt gift?*

Mom smiled and said, "Just wait and see."

Then Godmother Bernice stepped out and came back into the house with the biggest gift Victoria had ever seen! It had a huge sign with the words *The Greatest Gift of All.*

"The clue is in the gift!" Victoria screamed. She opened the clue sheet that was attached and read it aloud: "What was the name of the baby born on Christmas Day to bring hope, peace, and love to mankind?"

Victoria shouted excitedly, "Jesus!"

Victoria struggled to place the big box under the tree. She jumped in celebration of completing the scavenger hunt.

Merry
Christmas
The Greatest
Gift Of
All

Late on Christmas Eve, Victoria could not go to sleep as she pondered her last scavenger hunt gift. She thought, *What is inside that big box?*

Mom came in to kiss her good night and encouraged her to go to sleep. As she tucked Victoria in, she said, “Remember, tomorrow is Christmas Day, so there’s no need to think too much about the big box. You’ll find out soon enough!”

Victoria awoke the next morning to the smell of hot chocolate—yum! She shot out of the bed.

"It is Christmas Day!" she shouted with glee, and bolted for the Christmas tree. She looked at the big box and thought, *I cannot wait to open this great big gift!*

Mom interrupted her thoughts with a gentle pat and a nudge to sit with her on the couch. It was customary for the family to remember the Christmas story and give thanks for the true meaning of Christmas. Mom directed Victoria to the story in the Bible, and she began to read:

> "Today in the town of David a Savior has been born to you; he is the Messiah, the Lord. This will be a sign to you: You will find a baby wrapped in cloths and lying in a manger."

Reading the story of Christmas calmed Victoria and took her mind off the big box as she reflected on God's love for giving such a wonderful gift to the world!

After reflection time, Victoria scurried toward the Christmas tree and pulled out the Greatest Gift of All box. She quickly removed the wrapping paper and opened the box, which required some help from Mom.

Inside the box were sports clothes, dresses, shoes, ribbons, and a tiara! She was outfitted with clothes and shoes for the entire year! But rather than being excited about all the beautiful things in the box, Victoria was amazed at the box itself. The box had two sections that looked like two playpens.

Victoria quickly positioned one side of the box flat on the ground, stepped in, and sat down with a beaming smile! Just then, Godmother Bernice came over.

"Where did you get this wonderful box, Godmother?" Victoria asked.

"Take a wild guess!" she said with a grin.

Victoria turned the box over and saw a picture of a huge fan. "A fan box?"

Godmother Bernice had recently replaced the fan in her home that had stopped working after a very hot summer.

"That is a really big fan!" Victoria exclaimed.

After all the gifts were opened, Victoria returned to her favorite gift—the Greatest Gift of All box.

By late afternoon, the box had been converted to a table so she could put together her new puzzles that she had received for Christmas.

Once all the puzzles were completed, the box became a resting place for toys. After a month, it became overcrowded, and Mom insisted that the toys be returned to where they belonged.

With the box now empty, Mom said, “Victoria, it is time to throw out the box.”

“Oh no!” she exclaimed with a desperate look. “I’m not finished playing with it yet.”

Mom decided to give her a little more time with the box but cautioned that it must go at some point.

“Thank you,” Victoria said happily.

Later that day, Victoria had another idea for the box: a car! She imagined herself racing down a grassy hill with the wind in her hair as she swerved left and right until she arrived at the bottom of the hill. This fantasy went on for several days until she thought of another idea for the wonderful box...

An ice cream shop! The idea seemed great to her, but she needed help to cut out the window because she was not allowed to use sharp tools.

"Mom!" shouted Victoria, running to the kitchen. "I need your help."

After she explained her idea, Mom agreed to assist with the project. Victoria finished writing down all the flavors she would offer—strawberry, orange, lemon, mint, blueberry, grape, bubble gum, and chocolate. She then drew a big ice cream cone with four of her flavors—strawberry, blueberry, lemon, and orange—to show what she was selling. Mom chuckled at her little entrepreneur in the making.

As mom completed the cutouts, she asked, “How much are the ice cream cones?”

Victoria proudly looked up and said, “Fifty cents to twenty dollars.”

Mom gasped and blurted out, “Twenty dollars!”

Victoria giggled. “It is for fun, Mom,” she said with a mischievous look. Mom chuckled and went to the kitchen.

ICE CREAM

When Mom returned, the ice cream shop was up and ready for business. Victoria had pulled out her cash register and play money, and was seated inside her ice cream shop with her head looking through the window. Mom laughed and made her order. Soon, other family members were invited to experience the ice cream shop with its interesting flavors.

ICE CREAM

Throughout the year, the Greatest Gift of All box had become a fixture in the house. Before long, it was almost Christmas time again, and the ice cream shop had never closed. Mom tried to discard the box several times but eventually became attached to it, too.

As Christmas Day approached, Victoria had one more idea for the Greatest Gift of All box. She could not imagine a more fitting purpose, and got to work breaking down her beloved ice cream shop. Once completed, she gathered her work supplies to make her greatest idea yet. The box had been a gift container, a puzzle table, a toy box, a car, an ice cream shop, and now...

A Manger!

Victoria gently pulled the manger next to the Christmas tree and called her mom to see her masterpiece. Mom smiled, hugged Victoria tightly, and said, "You made your special box into a very special place, and I am very proud of you, Victoria!"

Victoria beamed, feeling quite proud of her achievement and her mom's approval. As they stood looking at the manger scene, Victoria caught sight of a beautiful star shining in the night sky. It was the final touch to complement her final work with the box to remember the greatest gift of all that was given to mankind—a Savior, born in a manger on Christmas Day.

THE GREATEST GIFT OF ALL

CPSIA information can be obtained
at www.ICGtesting.com
Printed in the USA
LVHW071149221222
735763LV00011B/416